Love's Rubber Armor

Thaïs Hardison

Copyright © 2015 by Thaïs Hardison Hinton
Illustrations by Ted Nunes
Cover Design by Octagon Labs

All rights reserved. This book or any portion therof may not be reproduced or used in any manner whatsoever without the express written permission of the publisher except for the use of brief quotations in a book review.

Printed in the United States of America
First Printing 2015

ISBN 978-0692429648

Library of Congress Control Number: 2015906065

Thaishardisonsonnets.com   UNITED STATES
Charleston, South Carolina, USA
thais@thaishardisonsonnets.com

Table of Contents

Sonnets of Love	1
Sonnets of Loss	22
Naughty Sonnets	33
Of Cabbages and Kings	47
Index	v

List of Figures

Entwife	62
Mrs. Claus	48
Nude reclined	34
nude kneeling	4
nude reclined 3	9
nude reclining	18
nude standing	38
Ophelia	53
Titania	57

ns of Love

The red of love too quickly fades to blue
The fever of love fades away too fast
And leaves not embers but a lonely hue
So tell me please, how do I make love last?
I invite love in but it never stays
Impatient, always looking at the door
It leaves me in an unrequited haze
The pangs of which I can hardly ignore
My heart is free and therefore prone to flee
Because my heart is light it flies from me
Acts like the moon, is governed by the sea
A moon that stays full I have yet to see
I'd rid myself of this Doppler Effect
If my free heart to earth I could connect

If one picture is worth a thousand words
Then I should paint a picture of your face
Instead of sending words to you in herds
Which poorly describe your beauty's fair grace
Forgive me for I cannot paint at all
Cannot outline with brush your loveliness
No picture can depict how you enthrall
Or how your smile seems to incandesce
My canvas is this poor, imperfect rhyme
My paint is just my pining for your arms
Your portrait would be beauty's paradigm
And reflect to you all your graceful charms
Your don't believe you're gorgeous, but you are
Of my desire, you're the avatar.

I wish you came more often and left less

Though if you're going to come you have to leave

Your absences I wish I could compress

Or from the time you're gone some minutes cleave

Every second you're away feels as though

It had been multiplied a thousand fold

If I could obviate your need to go

Or on the hands of time exert some hold

I hold only patience as I ponder

How by my side you could forever stay

Yet you have feet that are wont to wander

I somehow doubt that I will get my way.

I will not pen you, tell you not to go

Although I wish your return were less slow

With a bare eyeball, it hurts to see you

Your beauty is so great it pains my eyes

I'm speechless and I know not how to woo

Instead of words, I offer only sighs

Your beauty is so great I dare not dream

Of how your skin feels; your kiss; your embrace

But aggressive a lady must not seem

If only I'd not seen you I'd efface

The pace of my pulse when you are so near

Your beauty fills my eyes and numbs my brain

It draws me in but yet it keeps me far

I must not fall for you, I must stand clear

You are a cup from which I must refrain

Two edged; your beauty is both boon and bar.

If I said you were gorgeous I would lie

You have more cute than all of gorgeous owns

My language is not large enough to ply

My dear, my friend, you're pretty in your bones

To say that you are charming is untrue

Your charms disarm the meaning of the word

They overflow what the word would construe

Charm like yours has hitherto been unheard.

To call you smart would hardly be the truth

Clever, witty, sharp; they are all too weak

You have a unique genius sir, forsooth

Married quite well with an attitude meek

You may infer I think you're rather swell

My mind does choose to often on you dwell.

My words fall short of what I mean to say

My joy is inexpressible, complete

I lack the wit in words to woo you, pray

Forgive me for my lack of phrases sweet

For there are none as sacred as yourself

The strongest words I know seem much too weak

For you eclipse language itself

The unabridged does not hold what I seek

There are no terms for this, my huge emotion

If I say "love" I do not say it all

Four letters can't communicate devotion

The word love is by far too tiny, small

Although constricted by the alphabet

That does not make my love less infinite.

So much better if I'd never met you

Had never seen the beauty of your face

Had never fallen prey to your voodoo

And did not long to feel your warm embrace

I only hope that you I can forget

Never to taste the sweetness of your kiss

I will be lucky if I have the wit

To close my heart to you and never miss

The silk of your skin brushing against mine

The harmony of your voice in my ear

The fullness of your lips, they are divine

The fierceness of your fire, which I fear

You hold my heart with sweetest tyranny

And from that bondage I've no wish to flee.

How glad am I that thought is not the crime

Else I'd have been convicted long ago

Adulterous thoughts rise every time

All the control I have still lets them show

Once upon a dream I've held you before

And felt the fire held within your arms

But that was long ago in Elsinore

How dare you hide in marriage all your charms?

I could never bed a married man

Perhaps that's why I want you even more

Yet on my fantasies I'll lay no ban

In reality I will let dogs snore

Forgive me if I hold you in my dreams

Because I know I'll never hear your screams.

When all's been said and done and this is through
When I have lain with you and gone away
I will need someone to get over you
I fear that you are in my heart to stay
I need someone to take away the sting
Of leaving you, the pain of your absence
Though what we had was no more than a fling
It may have been short but it was intense
And so I need some balm to calm my mind
I need to let you fade into the night
I fear I will measure all other men
Compared to you them lacking do I find
No other lips I kiss will seem quite right
I need to scheme to be with you again.

How long do you suppose our love will last?
Will it be like a dream, both short and sweet?
Does love quick to arrive leave quite as fast?
Or will it last as long as lives complete?
I would not love you less if it were brief
I am content to love you just the same
I worry that it will all come to grief
Although this worry is a pointless game
It doesn't matter how long it will last
I will not count the minutes of content
I'll only count contentment whole, amassed
With you I'll not repent the minutes spent
I will not worry now, I'll wait to weep
If our love is a dream, then let me sleep.

I've given up trying to work today
Because I cannot chase you from my mind
These images appear and want to stay
Images that I wish I could unwind
They only haunt me now so far from you
And taunt me with their promise unfulfilled
My fantasies that one day will come true
Simply distract me. I am not iron-willed
My thoughts run to you every time I'm free
You're firmly in my brain – each nerve and cell
And I think about what is yet to be
Your lips, your eyes, your arms that I know well
I want you in whatever part of me
Can hold you love as long as I can see.

You cook with care, great knowledge and much skill
Serving fish steamed with white wine and grilled leeks
Over rice and yet it takes all my will
To focus on my plate and not your cheeks.
Mushrooms and gravy and tender beef tips
Offer corn in an orange reduction...
The best things at the table are your lips,
Along with my schemes for your seduction.
You marinate steaks in Guinness five days!
Good cuts paired with garlic mashed potatoes,
Yet all that I can taste are your sweet ways
And dream of gently nibbling on your nose.
You roast me with each look you give my eyes.
I'm seasoned with my blushes and my sighs.

Forgive me, though I have no rose for you
For if I did the rose would bow in shame
You have beauty, the rose, just residue
The world did not know lovely till you came
I do not have a box of chocolate sweets
One does not bring the honey to the bee
Chocolate would just taste sour next to thee
Your lips are tastier than any treats.
I have none of the standard valentines
But I don't want to give you standard love
For you I had to find a gift condign
A gift that is, I hope, a cut above
So, you may have me, body, mind, and heart
I love you so much we must never part.

I can't kiss you as often as I should
Each kiss you give me makes me yearn for more
Your body against mine you feel so good
Your kiss will keep me knocking at your door.
I always want to spend some time with you
It's always fun, both in and out of bed
I'm ready for you, there's no need to woo
You made it past my walls, you're in my head
I long for your embrace most every day
We must be careful, must not meet too much
I wish I could just one night with you stay
And wake up to your most expert sweet touch
We can't have that, so we should take tonight
And be together as much as we might.

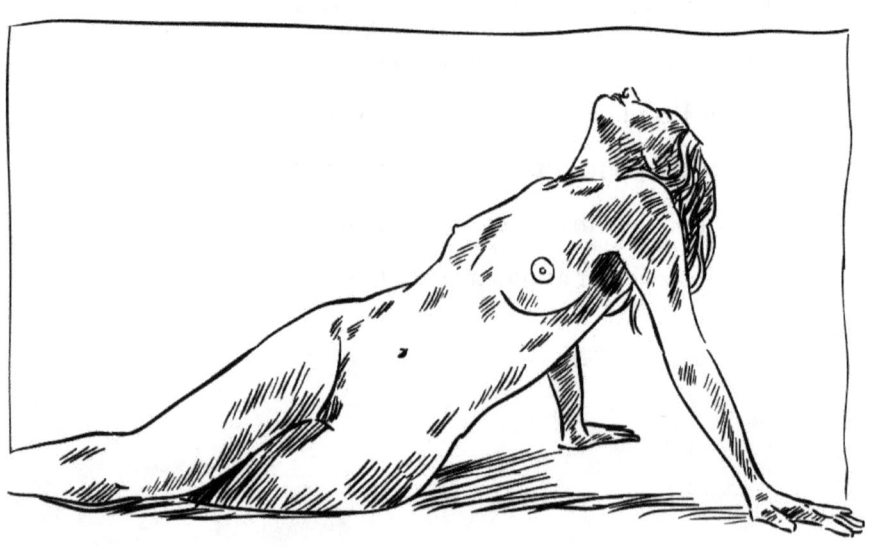

I want to wind around you one more time
To feel again your most excellent kiss
To quiver with your rhythm is sublime
Your lips and eyes and arms are those I miss.
I cannot see you every single day
Although I'd like to I can't work it out
I hold you in my mind and there you stay
Until I find some ruse to be about
Time I spend with you is never wasted
No matter if you hold me or we drink
Yours the finest lips I've ever tasted
Can't get enough of you is what I think.
I will not see you for about a week
But after that your company I'll seek.

I cannot see you for seven long days
Until then I'll survive on memories
Desire for you has me in a haze
I long to be with you I beg you please
Give me tonight so I can last a week
Without your sweet touch or your expert kiss
Two hours of your time is what I seek
Your arms your eyes your kisses I will miss
If I can get a kiss or two from you
Against the week your kiss will fortify
Me to survive without you all those nights
How I'm to last without you I've no clue
My heart's desire you personify
Each little thing you do to me delights.

I did not need a man to be complete
I told you as much in very plain talk
I told you of my faults on our first meet
Hoping for rejection; that you'd balk
Expecting that you'd rip my heart from me
And so you did but not the way I thought
Instead you hold my heart most carefully
And in your care I am most neatly caught
I need you more than food or drink or air
You haunt the very hallways of my mind
Imbued your love into my every breath
Also, I know you're needful of my care
You've given eyes to love, she is not blind
And I will love you even after death.

Sonnets of Loss

There is a soul-deep sadness in my heart
A melancholy that saps all my strength
My sadness springs from seconds we're apart
They seem stretched out to an infinite length
Each day away from you seems like a year
But yet you're in my mind's eye all the time
I almost hear you whisper in my ear
So sweet your voice like sussurant chime
When I am by your side time seems to fly
And hours turn to seconds in your gaze
You've got my senses wrapped up in a daze
Since one emotion you personify
Although you may have addled my poor brain
The love within my heart for you is plain.

I am filled with a sorrow I can't evade

She sleeps within the arms that should be mine

I do not think my woe will ever fade

She knows my intentions are not benign

At least, they are not from her perspective

You are her heart whom it would hurt to free

But if you choose to view the objective

I am a better mate for you than she

Our love reaches our hearts and minds and soul

She can't even give you conversation

Keep a cup of joy, or an empty bowl?

She loves you not with my adoration

I know that leaving her will hurt you too

But I have much more love to give to you.

You used to hold me treasured above all
There was no other woman you loved more
But you were shy then, and not quite so tall
My love, where was my error? Do I snore?
I did not seek your favor, ersatz love
And yet I still received it, all the same
I can't unlearn; you fit me like a glove
Now domesticated, my man is tame
You used to write me poetry, so shy
Poems that I keep, re-read, and treasure,
Alas, the milk is spilled, now I can cry
No other man can quite match your measure
My dear, I would have loved you well for years
My sorrow is too deep for simple tears.

Your friendship is a blessing and a curse
I'm still in love with you, I can't ignore
Forget, regret, or learn not to adore
In fact, I can't decide which fate is worse
To ban you from my sight, my hurts to fade
Would be a double loss, both friends and mates
To keep you as a friend, one hurt is stayed
Meanwhile the other hurt accumulates.
Your visage, in my eyes, both balm and bane
Love heavy in my throat like unshed tears
But to my closest friend that hurt unsaid
My heart is gone, and yet the ache remains
Your total absence is my greatest fear
Forcing me to accept friendship instead.

My calendar proclaims the start of spring
And daily does the sun increase his worth
Encouraging the flowers upward fling
Yet still the hand of winter fondles earth
Ebbing with a touch so slow to leave
Like Romeo who lingered to spite dawn
Slower than the lowest gear of grief
This winter tiptoes back across my lawn
To the inexorable I remain blind
Indifferent to the changing of the clime
Despite the birds announcement of the time
The lack of you around my senses bind
Without you I have no hope or reason
To acknowledge this slow change of season

I tell myself it is the snow today

Frozen water, steamless, blank as slate

The sky so grey, unblinking, and remote

The frigid winds who howl towards my door

I tell these lies so that I can ignore

The tears that try to climb up past my throat

Your life from mine was ripped; did bifurcate

It must just be this snow, or so I say

It is your absence that destroys my joy

Without your smile it's winter in my heart

I am lost without the love that you impart

I freeze in cold that nothing can alloy

Oh love; this lie is easier and so

There's nothing wrong with me, it's this damn snow!

Perhaps if I had loved you any less
I could have kept you – bided all the days
Instead I own a grief I can't redress
Exiled from you we went our separate ways
I should have praised your talents even more
Or if I could have wooed you with more wit
And written sonnets to you by the score
My sore regret would not here with me sit
You're farther from me with each passing year
Though when I close my eyes I feel your skin
And still remember how sweet was your kiss
I've no choice but to hold you ever dear
For among men there's none who is your twin
You are the mead – all other men are piss.

I will not write you sonnets anymore
If bothering to read them is too great
A task for you too tedious, a bore
I'll use simpler ways to communicate
I can appreciate that you're busy
But to forget that it was there at all
You don't have a bubble head, it's fizzy
There is no better way to make me small
Neither my love nor my sonnets are light
I'll make you immortal, you have a choice
Love or scorn can tint my poetic voice
So tell me, is my love a boon or bane?
You have my heart; make sure you treat it right.
Love held within a wounded heart will wane.

I will lose the memory of your touch
Your eyes your lips the soft touch of your arms
Cruel time will take my memories and much
More from me. Who am I without your charms?
A hollow shell aping all the moves that
Normal people make in reality
But these motions only make me feel flat
I need your love it is a surety.
I am too far from you and I wither
A remedy that I could surely solve.
By getting closer, flying into you
I need no kisses, I will not dither
Around your being I will soon revolve.
I cannot help but be in love with you.

Your sweetness bruised my soul but now you're gone

Removed from my life like you never came

Yet I still hope that we could carry on

Because without you I won't be the same

All other men can never quite compare

You stand above, apart from all the rest

The wildest dreams with you I dared to dare

To think of being yours myself I jest

Of my company you soon grew tired

Leery of lingering too long in place

And now I see you just in memory

It is as if the goose had quit the chase

The origin of all my discontent

Is that I still continue to lament.

Naughty Sonnets

I've known you for a while, we get along
I trust you not to talk behind my back
You have a sense of what is right and wrong
I think it's time we climbed into the sack.
Perhaps we could be friends with benefits
If I could steal some time to be with you
I'd lay with you as much as time permits
No strings attached, please do not misconstrue
We'd have to sneak around – be on the low
Weekends would be hard for me to arrange
I'll come to you as often as I can.
The first time we will take it nice and slow
Sleeping together is the only change
I hope you will say yes to my sweet plan.

I use my intelligence to seduce

Inducing you to quell my deep desire

I take my time leaving you to deduce

The where, how and when that I conspire

To see my design satisfied at last

But I unwilling to rush to mingle

To savor sex one must not move too fast

Tired of tossing in my bed single

I wish to swish my skin with your sweet sweat

Wet am I with the mere idea of it

Will you not become my sexual pet?

Just ask, and upon your face I will sit

You infer this sonnet was just a ruse

To grace my bed for this night you I choose.

I long to feel your touch between my thighs

And your shy fingers on my quivering breast

Weary of undressing you with my eyes

I would take you to bed, but not to rest

Horizontally I pine to entwine

I hunger for nibbles I can't digest

My urgent desire you do define

Won't you satisfy my body's unrest?

I will burn up in anticipation

Is it your intention to make me plead?

Please join with me now in fornication

I want you to mount me and take the lead

To my advances please do not resist

Trust me to lead you to a state of bliss.

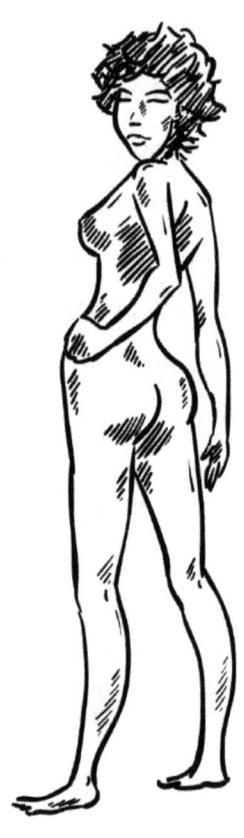

I dream of what your bare skin would feel like
As your body dips, slips inside of mine
Would it be best to ride you like a bike
Or should you enter me while you're behind
And grab my hips as deeper in you thrust?
Thoughts of your cock make me tingly and weak
So I'd prefer to face your naked lust
The first time in my thighs for hide and seek
But I can only arch my back and moan
After tasting your essence on my lips
Hearing you gasp and pant and beg and groan
Hard to decide how best to join our hips
I rob my sleep to reflect on your charms
Because I cannot rest inside your arms.

You tied me up but then you let me go
Teaching me how carefree you really are
Now I possess no rope rash left to show
It has been weeks since I have seen your car
In my driveway. My feet I want tied tight
I have the right to ask you at least that
I hope to be invited for the night
Indifferent, you just ask for me to scat
That is a habit engendered, I'm sure
For your protection. It is romantic
To wake up side by side. You never were
Fond of relationships that are static
When you know that it takes two you will frown
One to be tied up, one to be tied down.

I had secrets that I kept from myself
Things that I thought were only fantasy
But yesterday I discovered the wealth
Of letting her into bed with me
I knew her body like I know my own
It was my first time but I still found
All secret places that would make her moan
Her groans arose from her secret playground
Heating we dissolved in sensual hues
Blending like the softest strokes of paint
Innocent brown eyes mix with boiling blues
Honey, I know of sin and this it ain't
I satisfied her, gave her some release
She fell asleep still wearing her chemise.

I have to think about you every day
Foolishly changing my password at work
I chose your name. It was my silly way
Of expressing my wishes. Now you lurk
Inside my brain and cause such dreams to come
Dreams that I will act on when I see you.
Until that time to pleasure I am numb
I have to wait until that time we do
Those things that make me shiver with delight
I'm hungry for your touch again my dear
Our timing has not always been the best
But I will travel far to set it right
I have a mission, my destiny's clear
I mean to put your body to the test.

I long to taste the touch of your sweet lips
And feel your body move beneath my hand
I want to wear the full weight of your hips
On mine, grinding to make your big self stand
Erect, and harder than you've ever been
I'd like to peel your clothes off with much haste
Kneeling before you, my lips would begin
To embrace your sex. Hungry for your taste
I'd suck you deep and feel you in my throat
I want to suck you to the very brink
If I got any wetter I would float
You get me so hot I can't even think
I'm wild to feel you thrust between my thighs
And be surrounded by your groans and sighs.

There is a fever raging in my breast

A fever only your two lips can cure

Of all my lovers I like you the best

The way you touch me is so right, so sure.

You say you're only being observant

There's magic in your touch I am convinced

Your wish is my task I am your servant

The way you love me is superb, intense.

I cannot get enough of your sweet kiss

I want you when I sleep and when I wake

The way you move inside me causes bliss

I'm worried too much time of yours I take

My pleasure is your target and you score

You love me so well I keep wanting more.

I can't wait to have your cock inside me

For you to fuck me like you love to do

I love to fuck you too, so we agree

I love your penis and how big it grew

When you are in my mouth you're at my throat

I love to suck you so that you come hard

You make me come so much that I could float

Your fingers and your lips do so bombard

I want you in my pussy every day

We fuck a lot but still I want some more

I want to fuck you in every way

You love to fuck so you I do adore

I cannot get enough of your sweet cock

When you fuck me you make my whole world rock

I thought we would just have some fun in bed
I did not know how good your kiss could be
And now you are embedded in my head
I cannot wait to hold you inside me
But wait I must, I cannot see you yet
I cannot hold you in my arms today
Anticipation is making me wet
I have to wait until this Saturday
I need to be within your arms again
I need to feel your kiss upon my lips
I like you best among all of the men
I need to feel you deep inside my hips
I want to feel your kisses every day
I've fallen for you, as I feared I may

Of Cabbages and Kings

A city girl, who thought it would be slow
Living north of Narnia, could I last?
Good logic had he for wanting to go
But in a week years sink into the past
We work and woo so hard we lose ourselves
Like frost on windowpanes our edges blur
Just us, some reindeer and nine jolly elves
The seasons twist and turn all in a whirr
December is his favorite season
But I myself prefer summer's fine heat
Yet loving him gives me every reason
To cherish winter; it makes him complete.
Although north of my ideal location
With him I stay in satiation.

People do anything to waste the time
As if it were grime to be washed away
Folks just do not realize how sublime
Is time, one needs to try to make it stay.
The sway of years makes tears of boredom rise
Though boredom is a fairly recent word
A basic scarcity makes it unwise
To throw time away surely is absurd
You cannot throw away what you can't touch
There are those who say, "I have time to kill"
But they are ignorant of things as such
I want to say I have time to distil
You can't kill time, with me you must agree
Only done by harming eternity

As long as I have eyes left in my head
It will always shock me to see you eat
That modern myth of goodness: wonder bread
Which is not junk but it is not complete
Unreal light without luminosity
They call it wholesome but it is not whole
It has thickness but not viscosity
Substance with no matter, it has no soul
Don't you desire a more substantive slice?
A nice loaf laden with all that is sweet
White bread is no value at any price
Bran and germ from grain they should not delete
If you eat white bread, yourself you will cheat
Instead nibble on the brunette, whole wheat.

It's so hard to shut down and go seek sleep
When life is so big and time is so small
Consciousness is precious, so sweet to keep
Sixteen hours are too brief; I want them all
One third of our lives we spend in stasis
That fraction sacrificed for sanity
The body can't be denied that basis
The loss of time is a profanity
What is sleep but a small taste of our doom?
Your mind time warps from night right on to day
Fleeting we find our grave straight from the womb
Sleep is a simile so that we may
Never forget that our days here are few
Yet we've an endless choice of things to do.

Do not attempt to take me from my mood

There are no pleasures I can be drawn to

I simply want to sit, and sulk, and brood

Indigo is depression deepest blue

There is no course of action I can take

No moral action nor a legal one

He will not marry for the baby's sake

He says it wasn't love we had, but fun

I'm sure things would be different were he sane

His dad alive, and his succession sure

I didn't think his love would ever wane

There was no need for that nunnery slur.

I'd rather have death than life without him

Let everyone think that I could not swim.

I have tried to write sonnets; I cannot
My words do not flow freely on the page
With ineptitude my poor rhymes are fraught
I do not have the wit with words to wage
A fourteen line, metered conversation
Past attempts have been stuttering stumbles
I sink into iambic frustration
Like an imperfect actor who mumbles
I've no wish to abridge my ideas to fit
Constricted to that inflexible box
Yet I keep attempting, I will not quit
Wherefore this, my inherent paradox?
When I in sonnets do poetic wax
I acquire the structure that I do lack.

I'd rather have a friend than a lover

Though lovers can be nice and sometimes are

Friends are few; too many of the other

Yet on more lovers I will lay no bar

True friends are far more precious in my view

Like gemstones, whose worth is derived from lack

Rarity is a cause of great ado

Who doesn't need more friends to guard their back?

Lovers are a completely different breed

Friends can be lovers, lovers never friend

With friends you may talk, but lovers never heed

If friends become lovers, friendship will end

If lovers are weeds, friends are the crop

You may pick any weed, but for friends you must shop.

I shall not write you sonnets anymore

Nor shall I bring you laurels for your crown

If only you I let myself ignore

You are the air without which I will drown

I have pleaded with you to end this fight

The strife that throws the seasons from their pace

Why won't you dance with me and make things right?

You in my bed, the seasons in their place

You sent an ass to me, all for a lark

You thought this would destroy me, once I knew

Yet you don't see that Puck's pulled one on you

Your inner self on Bottom did he mark

I hope this is a glamour that you wear

Your indifference is what I cannot bear

Life seems like such a temporary thing

Compared to the great life spans of the spheres

So brief our dance alive; really a fling

So why remark the turn of all the years?

You celebrate the first year at the end

Call yourself one when you are starting two

Title of age to end of year suspend-

This idiosyncratic custom we do!

Our lives are just a sigh to mother Earth

Although we cherish each and every day

How insignificant is each year worth?

We're just composed of ground up rocks and clay.

So what is one more birthday in your life?

A chance to celebrate surviving strife!

My youth and beauty you have almost spent.

Treebeard you talk but never do a thing;

You who know so much my neutral Ent!

You used to make my roots and branches sing.

Young saplings do not fall out of the sky.

We cannot live as long as men folk do.

It seems I go unnoticed by your eye.

Treebeard, you're running out of time to woo.

I cannot remain here with you my love,

You make my roots feel like they're planted sand.

And now I must take wing a wounded dove...

To stay here kills me slowly. It's so dire!

I have no clue as to where I will land,

But I will move west nearer toward the Shire.

Treebeard my love I hope this finds you well.

I walked west toward the Shire for some three months

And now my roots feel like they've been through hell.

The soil is good here. Dear, I loved you once

And always will I long for you present.

I had to go. I hope you find my notes.

On my journey I saw no other Ent.

The sunlight is rich here and filled with motes.

I can live here although I'll live alone.

There is a river here I will survive

Treebeard, I miss you, Ent whom I adore.

My chance for children I have surely blown.

You never would have taken me to wive.

Time to send this note. Love, your sycamore.

I wonder why you never do write back.
One hundred years and not one word from you!
I guess you think me just some silly hack.
Treebeard you loved me once; thought you still do.
Your silence puzzles me. Have you not read
My letters, sent to you each year by squirrel?
Treebeard my love I hope you are not dead.
The elves have come to middle earth, they whirl
And caper round my trunk - such hasty things!
Their lives are shorter still than even mine
I hope this letter will reach you at last
Bees have settled in my trunk, the hive sings.
They cannot carry letters. How I whine!
I love you still, no matter what our past.

Index

A city girl, who thought it would be slow	49
As long as I have eyes left in my head	51
Do not attempt to take me from my mood	54
Forgive me, though I have no rose for you	16
How glad am I that thought is not the crime	11
How long do you suppose our love will last?	13
I am filled with a sorrow I can't evade	24
I can't kiss you as often as I should	17
I cannot see you for seven long days	20
I cannot wait to have your cock inside me	45
I did not need a man to be complete	21
I dream of what your bare skin would be like	39
I had secrets that I kept from myself	41
I have to think about you every day	42
I have tried to write sonnets; I cannot	55
I long to feel your touch between my thighs	37
I long to taste the touch of your sweet lips	43
I shall not write you sonnets anymore	58
I tell myself it is the snow today	28
I thought we would just have some fun in bed	46
I use my intelligence to seduce	36
I want to wind around you one more time	19
I will lose the memory of your touch	31
I will not write you sonnets anymore	30

I wish you came more often and left less	5
I wonder why you never do write back	63
I'd rather have a friend than a lover	56
I've given up trying to work today	14
I've known you for a while, we get along	35
If I said you were gorgeous I would lie	7
If one picture is worth a thousand words	3
It's so hard to shut down and go seek sleep	52
Life seems like such a temporary thing	59
My calendar proclaims the start of spring	27
My words fall short of what I mean to say	9
My youth and beauty you have almost spent	60
People do anything to waste the time	50
Perhaps if I had loved you any less	29
So much better if I'd never met you	10
The red of love too quickly fades to blue	2
There is a fever raging in my breast	44
There is a soul-deep sadness in my heart	23
Treebeard my love I hope this finds you well	61
When all's been said and done and this is through	12
With a bare eyeball, it hurts to see you	6
You cook with care, great knowledge, ...	15
You tied me up but then you let me go	40
You used to hold me treasured above all	25
Your friendship is a blessing and a curse	26
Your sweetness bruised my soul ...	32

www.ingramcontent.com/pod-product-compliance
Lightning Source LLC
Chambersburg PA
CBHW061342040426
42444CB00011B/3044